# CHICAGO BLACKHAWKS

## By Beth Adelman

**THE CHILD'S WORLD®**
1980 Lookout Drive • Mankato, MN 56003-1705
800-599-READ • www.childsworld.com

**ACKNOWLEDGMENTS**
The Child's World®: Mary Berendes, Publishing Director
Shoreline Publishing Group, LLC: James Buckley, Jr.,
    Production Director
The Design Lab: Gregory Lindholm, Design and
    Page Production

**PHOTOS**
Cover: Getty Images
Interior: AP/Wide World: 5, 6, 10, 17, 18, 21, 25 (3), 26, 27;
    Getty Images: 9, 13, 22

**LIBRARY OF CONGRESS**
**CATALOGING-IN-PUBLICATION DATA**
Adelman, Beth.
    Chicago Blackhawks / by Beth Adelman.
        p. cm.
    Includes bibliographical references and index.
    ISBN 978-1-60253-441-4 (library bound : alk. paper)
    1.  Chicago Blackhawks (Hockey team)—History—Juvenile
literature.  I. Title.

GV848.C48A34 2010
796.962'640977311—dc22

2010015296

Printed in the United States of America
Mankato, Minnesota
July 2010
F11538

# TABLE OF CONTENTS

# GO, BLACKHAWKS!

The crowd screams "Let's go, Hawks!" as the Chicago Blackhawks race down the ice. One player passes the **puck** to another. Suddenly, a Blackhawks skater shoots the puck toward the net. It blasts in for a Blackhawks goal! The Blackhawks win! The players jump up and hug each other. Let's meet the Chicago Blackhawks!

The Chicago Blackhawks celebrate another goal.

Blackhawks **defenseman** Duncan Keith protects the puck from a San Jose Sharks player.

# WHO ARE THE CHICAGO BLACKHAWKS?

The Chicago Blackhawks play in the National Hockey League (NHL). They are one of 30 teams in the NHL. The NHL includes the Eastern Conference and the Western Conference. The Blackhawks play in the Central Division of the Western Conference. The playoffs end with the winners of the Eastern and Western conferences facing off. The champion wins the **Stanley Cup**. The Blackhawks have won four Stanley Cups.

7

# WHERE THEY CAME FROM

The Blackhawks joined the NHL in 1926. They are one of the Original Six—the league's first teams. The team was named after the U.S. Army's Blackhawk Division. The team's first owner was an officer in that division in World War I. The Blackhawks won their first Stanley Cup in 1934. They won again in 1938. Then they had to wait 23 years for another championship. That year, they were lead by two of the greatest players ever: Bobby Hull and Stan Mikita.

Bobby Hull (left) was the NHL's top goal-scorer seven times. He was a key player when the Blackhawks won the Stanley Cup in 1961.

The Blackhawks and the Detroit Red Wings pile up on the puck.

# WHO THEY PLAY

The Chicago Blackhawks play 82 games each season. They play all the other teams in their division six times. The other Central Division teams are the Nashville Predators, the Detroit Red Wings, the St. Louis Blues, and the Columbus Blue Jackets. The Blackhawks and the Red Wings are fierce **rivals**. The Blackhawks also play other teams in the Western and Eastern Conferences.

11

# WHERE THEY PLAY

The Blackhawks play their home games in the United Center. They moved to their new **arena** in 1995. Before that, they played at Chicago Stadium. When Chicago Stadium was built in 1929, it was the biggest sports arena in the country. Over the years, newer, bigger arenas were built. By the time Chicago Stadium was torn down, it was one of the smallest in the country.

In 2009, the Blackhawks played a game outdoors! They faced the Red Wings in a game at Wrigley Field in Chicago.

13

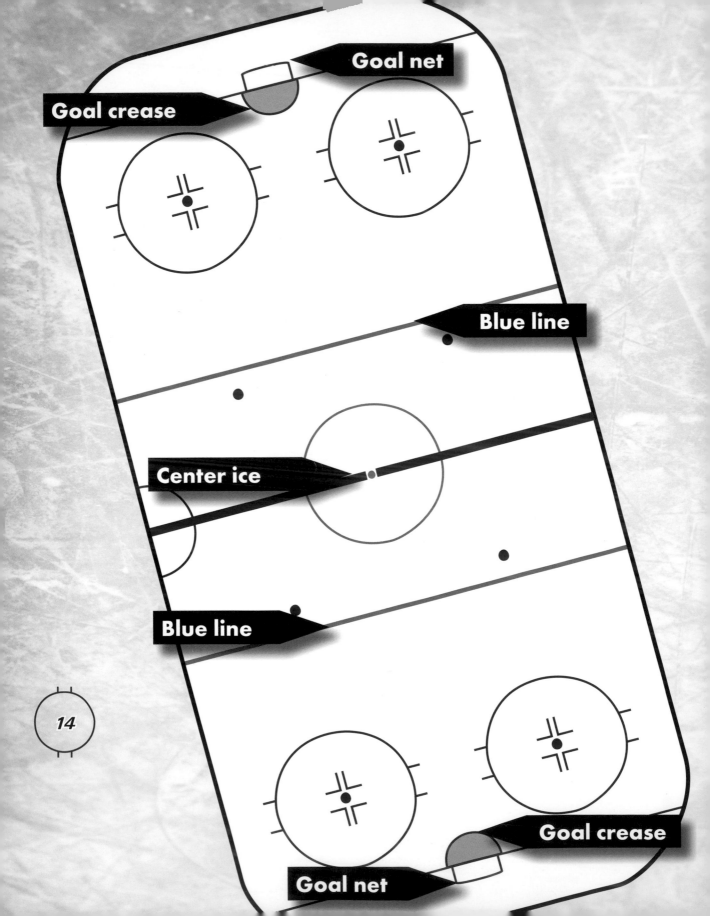

Goal net

Goal crease

Blue line

Center ice

Blue line

Goal crease

Goal net

14

# THE HOCKEY RINK

Hockey games are played on a sheet of ice called a rink. It is a rounded rectangle. NHL rinks are 200 feet (61 m) long and 85 feet (26 m) wide. Wooden boards surround the entire rink. Clear plastic panels are on top of the boards so fans can see the action and be protected from flying pucks. Netting is hung above the seats at each end of the rink to catch any wild pucks. The goal nets are near each end of the rink. Each net is four feet (1.2 m) high and six feet (1.8 m) wide. A red line marks the center of the ice. Blue lines mark each team's defensive zone.

## THE PUCK

An NHL puck is made of very hard rubber. The disk is three inches (76 mm) wide and 1 inch (25 mm) thick. It weighs about 6 ounces (170 g). It's black so it's easy to see on the ice. Many pucks are used during a game, because some fly into the stands.

15

# BIG DAYS!

The Blackhawks have had many great seasons in their long history. Here are three of the greatest:

**1933–34: Goalie** Charlie Gardiner was a key player when the Blackhawks won their first Stanley Cup. Gardiner was named the best goalie in the NHL that year.

**1960–61:** After 23 years without a Stanley Cup, the Blackhawks finally won the championship again. They beat their rivals, the Red Wings, to do it! That season, the Blackhawks set a team record for wins and **points**.

**2009–10:** The Blackhawks won the Stanley Cup! They were the best team in the league all season, then they fought through the playoffs. In the Stanley Cup finals, they beat the Philadelphia Flyers to win the title.

Patrick Kane lifts the Stanley Cup the Blackhawks won in 2010.

The St. Louis Blues knocked the
Blackhawks out of the playoffs in 2002.

18

# TOUGH DAYS!

The Blackhawks won their last Stanley Cup in 1961. Here are some of the toughest times in team history.

**1946–47 through 1959–60:** For 15 years, the Blackhawks had a losing regular-season record. That means they lost more games than they won.

**1991–92:** The Blackhawks finished second overall in the NHL and went to the Stanley Cup Finals. But they lost four games in a row to the Pittsburgh Penguins.

**1997–98 through 2007–08:** The Blackhawks made it to the playoffs only once in 11 seasons.

# MEET THE FANS

Blackhawks fans are known for being very loud. They start cheering while the team is warming up! After many difficult seasons, fans have a lot to cheer about these days. The Chicago Blackhawks have one of the youngest teams in the NHL. Their fans love this new group of great players. The Blackhawks have set NHL attendance records for several seasons. Fans can also finally follow their team on TV. For a long time, they could only watch Blackhawks games at the arena.

The Blackhawks fans gave their team a Stanley Cup parade in 2010!

21

In 1960, Bobby Hull (left) and Stan Mikita (right) celebrate Hull's 200th NHL point. Hull scored the most goals ever for the Blackhawks. Mikita had the second most.

# HEROES THEN...

Many players in the **Hockey Hall of Fame** wore the red, black, and white Blackhawks colors. Greats such as left **wing** Bobby Hull and **center** Stan Mikita played at the same time. Both were amazing scorers. Hull was known for being lightning-fast and super-strong. In 1968-69, Hull scored 58 goals in one season—an NHL record. He was named the Most Valuable Player (MVP) two years in a row. Then Mikita was MVP the next two years! Mikita was also the NHL's top scorer four times. Center Denis Savard was known for his tricky spinning moves. He was super-fast and a top scorer. Tony Esposito has the most wins of any Blackhawks goalie. The team made the playoffs every season that he was in goal.

23

# HEROES NOW...

The Blackhawks today have some of the best players in the NHL. In 2007, center Jonathan Toews scored his first NHL goal on his first shot in his first game! The next season, he was named the team **captain**—at just 20 years old! Also in 2007, right wing Patrick Kane finished the season with the most points for any NHL **rookie**. He was named the NHL's best rookie player. Duncan Keith is known as a two-way defenseman. That means he stops other teams from scoring, but also scores a lot of goals. Toews and Keith played for Canada in the 2010 Winter Olympics. Kane played in the Olympics for the United States.

CENTER

JONATHAN TOEWS

RIGHT WING

PATRICK KANE

DEFENSEMAN

DUNCAN KEITH

25

# GEARING UP

Hockey players wear short pants and a jersey called a "sweater." Underneath, they wear lots of pads to protect themselves. They also wear padded gloves and a hard plastic helmet. They wear special ice hockey skates with razor-sharp blades. They carry a stick to handle the puck.

Goalies wear special gloves to help them block and catch shots. They have extra padding on their legs, chest, and arms. They also wear special decorated helmets and use a larger stick.

26

Customized helmet

Catching glove

Blocker

Goalie stick

Leg pads

Skates with blocking blades

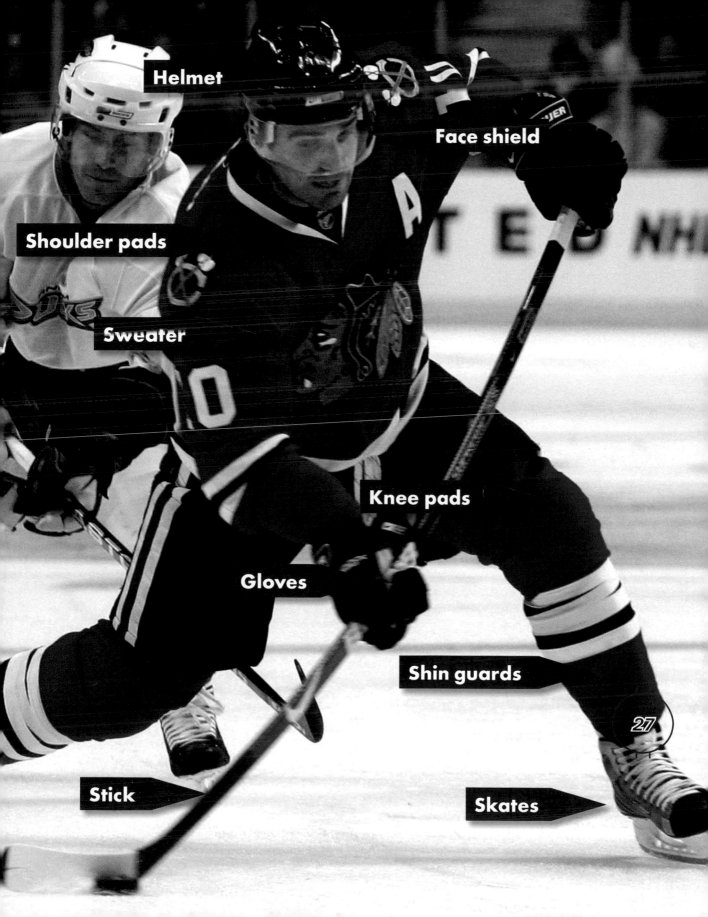

Helmet

Face shield

Shoulder pads

Sweater

Knee pads

Gloves

Shin guards

Stick

Skates

27

# SPORTS STATS

Here are some all-time career records for the Chicago Blackhawks. All the stats are through the 2009–2010 season.

## HOT SHOTS

### GOALS

These players have scored the most career goals for the Blackhawks.

| PLAYER | GOALS |
| --- | --- |
| Bobby Hull | 604 |
| Stan Mikita | 541 |

## PERFECT PASSERS

### ASSISTS

These players have the most career **assists** on the team.

| PLAYER | ASSISTS |
| --- | --- |
| Stan Mikita | 926 |
| Denis Savard | 719 |

## BIG SCORES!

### POINTS

These players have the most points, a combination of goals and assists.

| PLAYER | POINTS |
| --- | --- |
| Stan Mikita | 1,467 |
| Bobby Hull | 1,153 |

## SUPER SAVERS

### GOALS AGAINST AVERAGE

These Chicago goalies have allowed the fewest goals per game in their career.

| PLAYER | GAA |
|---|---|
| Charlie Gardiner | 2.02 |
| Glenn Hall | 2.60 |

## PLAYER POSITIVE

### CAREER PLUS-MINUS

These players have the best **plus-minus** in Blackhawks history.

| PLAYER | PLUS-MINUS |
|---|---|
| Steve Larmer | +182 |
| Bill White | +176 |

## FROM THE BENCH

### COACHES

These coaches have the most wins in Blackhawks history.

| COACH | WINS |
|---|---|
| Billy Reay | 516 |
| Bob Pulford | 185 |

# GLOSSARY

**arena** an indoor place for sports

**assist** a play that gives the puck to the player who scores a goal

**captain** a player chosen to lead his team on and off the ice

**center** a hockey position at the middle of the forward, offensive line

**defenseman** a player who takes a position closest to his own goal, to keep the puck out

**goalie** the goaltender, whose job is to keep pucks out of the net

**Hockey Hall of Fame** located in Toronto, Ontario, this museum honors the greatest players in the sport's history

**plus-minus** a player gets a plus one for being on the ice when their team scores a goal, and a minus one when the other team scores a goal; the total of these pluses and minuses creates this stat. The better players always have high plus ratings

**points** a team gets two points for every game they win and one point for every game they tie; a player gets a point for every goal he scores and another point for every assist

**puck** the hard, frozen rubber disk used when playing hockey

**rivals** teams that play each other often and with great intensity

**rookie** a player in his first season in a pro league

**Stanley Cup** the trophy awarded each year to the winner of the National Hockey League championship

**wing** a hockey position on the outside left or right of the forward line

# FIND OUT MORE

## BOOKS

Skog, Jason. *The Story of the Chicago Blackhawks*. Toronto: Saunders Book Co., 2009.

Stewart, Mark. *Chicago Blackhawks: Team Spirit*. Chicago: Norwood House Press, 2009.

Thomas, Kelly, and John Kicksee. *Inside Hockey!: The Legends, Facts, and Feats that Made the Game*. Toronto: Maple Leaf Press, 2008.

## WEB SITES

Visit our Web page for links about the Chicago Blackhawks and other pro hockey teams.

*childsworld.com/links*

Note to Parents, Teachers, and Librarians: We routinely verify our Web links to make sure they are safe, active sites—so encourage your readers to check them out!

# INDEX

## ABOUT THE AUTHOR

Beth Adelman thinks hockey is the greatest sport in the world. She used to live in Chicago and still cheers for the Blackhawks. She has written and edited dozens of books for young readers.